More Frontline Sketches

by Pat Turner

The BackYard Theatre Co.

MOORLEY'S Print & Publishing

ISBN 0 86071 397 0

MOORLEY'S Print & Publishing

23 Park Rd., Ilkeston, Derbys DE7 5DA

Tel/Fax: (0115) 932 0643

Foreword

Another collection of sketches containing some of our favourite characters; the long-suffering philosopher, Sydney, who doesn't say much but can get a lot of laughs through facial expressions, and William Morton, the cardboard cut-out cowboy. Our villain is made of hardwood, is lifesize and pasted over in newspaper, then dressed in cowboy hat, scarf and waistcoat. He is free-standing.

"The Price is Paid" works particularly well on the streets since William attracts a crowd on his own. Stand him near your space dressed in hat and waistcoat while you make your preparations and he will gain attention for you. This is helpful because it is better to gain a crowd, <u>then</u> do the sketch, rather than waste a clear message, performing to a few. Alternatively, bring William on ceremoniously to the banging of a drum, signalling his "march to the scaffold". This is just a device to catch the crowd's attention before the dialogue begins.

"Any Minute Now" has been used on the streets too. It lends itself to the use of a microphone.

"The Boxed Heart" is fast moving yet changes tempo at the end. We often follow it with a song to use the thoughtful mood created.

Pat Turner.

CONTENTS

ETERNAL LIFE!

(A News seller is shouting to sell his papers. Sydney and Agnes enter.)

NEWS: ETERNAL LIFE! ETERNAL LIFE! Get your ETERNAL LIFE here.....

AGNES: 'Ere, Sydney, what do you think?

SYDNEY: Looks like one of them mail-order catalogues to me - You know, you get your present free with your first order.

AGNES: What do you know about mail-order catalogues?
(She pokes him.)
I say, look at me when I'm talking to yer ..... What do you know about mail-order catalogues? We've never had one.

SYDNEY: *(To audience.)* I know about orders though!

NEWS: ETERNAL LIFE! Free today .....

SYDNEY: *(Waves to News seller.)* Hello.

AGNES: *(Pokes him.)* Don't talk to strangers Sydney; you never know who they are! *(She pushes him aside and goes to the News seller.)* Excuse me ..... What's the catch?

NEWS: There's no catch madam.

AGNES: No, I mean why is it free? I thought you had to earn things like that .....

NEWS: No madam, it's a free gift.

AGNES: Yes but, do I have to be good ..... because ..... I haven't always been perfect you know. *(Sydney nods in agreement.)* I shout at my husband and I ..... *(Whacks the News seller in a friendly manner.)* Well! If I stood here confessing to you all day I'd have a list as long as my arm ..... but I'm sure we all have a tale we could tell, don't we?

NEWS: I'm sure we do madam, I'm sure we do but don't worry, it's a free gift - whatever you've done, you still qualify ..... that is, if you're sorry .....

AGNES: Well, what do I have to do?

NEWS: Just ask and receive, love, ask and receive!

AGNES: Can I have it then?

NEWS: *(Gives her several papers with the titles written on them.)*
There we are love, - one brand new ETERNAL LIFE! Complete

5

with the set of LOVE, JOY, PEACE .....
(Agnes is over the moon, taking them and stuffing them in her carrier bag. She grabs the next one.)
.....PATIENCE, GOODNESS, KINDNESS and SELF-CONTROL!

AGNES: Oooh! I could do with a bit of self-control!

SYDNEY: *(To audience.)* She could an' all!
(Agnes belts him with the paper, then realises it is the SELF-CONTROL issue and stops. She moves away and looks through her papers. Sydney sidles up to the News seller.)
'Ere, have you got any more of that there self-control?

NEWS: Sorry Sir, we don't sell them separately ..... It's the full package or nothing.

SYDNEY: Where do you get your stuff from then?

NEWS: The Bible.

SYDNEY: The Bible eh?

AGNES: Sydney, come on, we haven't got all day!

SYDNEY: I know some of that.

NEWS: Do you Sir?

SYDNEY: I can quote it too.

NEWS: Really?

AGNES: Sydney, get over here and bring the bags!
(She scowls at him, then freezes, scowling at the audience.)

SYDNEY: *(Philosophises.)* A nagging wife is like a dripping tap - drip..... drip..... drip!

FIVE PUNK ROCKERS

(Five Punks stand in a line, glaring at the audience. The leader begins to stamp out a rhythm which is picked up by the gang. This is to set the tempo of the poem. The poem is choral speech, with all joining in the chorus, and individuals saying lines. At the end of each section a punk leaves the gang, quickly does something to signify he / she has left the image, e.g. wipes make up off or takes off a jacket, and continues the poem as an observer to the gang. In their actions, the punks show aggression, image, and depression. Since most lines are shouted by all, it is possible to use this on the street.)

LEADER:	*(Stamp, stamp, stamp.)*
ALL:	*(Stamp, stamp, stamp.)* FIVE PUNK ROCKERS, OUT TO WAGE A WAR.
1:	One had to sign on today. *(He leaves.)*
ALL:	And then there were four. Four punk rockers - "WE'RE THE POWERS THAT BE!"
2:	One had to fetch his baby bro'. *(He leaves.)*
ALL:	And then there were three.
3 PUNKS:	Three punk rockers, messin' in full view!
OBSERVER:	One got the huff on! *(One leaves.)*
ALL:	And then there were two.
2 PUNKS:	Two punk rockers, out to have some fun.
OBSERVER:	One felt depressed today. *(One leaves.)*
ALL:	And then there was one. One punk rocker.
OBSERVER 1:	Wondering what went wrong.
OBSERVER 2:	He'd never liked it anyway.
OBSERVER 3:	He'd only played along.

(The last one looks around. He is abandoned. He kneels and raises his hands in despair. Freeze.)

(The actions may be a series of pictures - instant freezes showing aggression, messing about, etc. Consider different levels and angles to make each picture interesting. There should be a distinct contrast between the punks and the sympathetic, understanding observers.)

THE BOXED HEART

(A fast-talking market trader enters, carrying an attractive looking box full of hearts of all sizes. He aims to sell the audience a bargain ..... but as the sketch progresses he loses his sales drive and begins to talk realistically, just telling people about Jesus.)

Gentlemen, what can you give your ladies this Valentine? *(Christmas / Anniversary.)*

We have for your delectation and delight, what every love is made of - THE BOXED HEART! ..... Comes in many types and sizes so we can be sure we have the right one for YOU.

(Produces first heart.) We have the stuffed heart - takes plenty of bashing ..... *(demonstrates)* and lasts for years ..... next we have the chocolate heart, and what lady doesn't love chocolate? ..... Yes madam, I know you do. *(demonstrates)* Looks lovely on the outside, *(opens it)* Hollow on the inside ..... however it does come in two halves ..... so you can keep half for yourself gents!

We have the plastic heart - made in Hong Kong ..... No feelings, but it works! ..... Or maybe you prefer the NEW, ECONOMY DISPOSABLE HEART! ..... When you've finished with your first love, you just THROW IT AWAY! ..... and get a new one - FREE!

BUT TONIGHT'S STAR BARGAIN is a real, beating, human heart. No ordinary heart this, Ladies and Gentlemen; in this heart you will find no lies, no hate, no jealousy, no pride ..... In this heart is peace, purity, truth, kindness, love - Yes, it's all about love this Valentine's ..... and this life-giving heart can be yours, free.

Guaranteed for eternity.

Broken for you.

TRUE VALENTINE

(Romeo is in traditional tights and blouse. Juliet is in modern dress. She is seething and pacing up and down, lovelorn, searching for Romeo.)

ROMEO: Sweet Valentine! (He is at the back of the hall waving a single rose. He prances artistically down the isle.

JULIET: Aha! *(She throws something at him. Direct hit.)*

ROMEO: What light through yonder window breaks? It is the east, and Juliet is the sun.

JULIET: *(Her speech is a cross between Shakespearean style and an angry woman.)*
Oh Romeo, Romeo, wherefore hast thou been, Romeo?
Thou art a full two hours late.
My heart beats sore - I'm in a right state.

ROMEO: I had to walk here, Juliet
Oh please don't make a fuss
The driver took one look at me
And threw me off the bus.

Pray pardon me, dear Juliet
Forgive me, dearest lamb
The cars all stopped as I passed by
I caused a traffic jam.

JULIET: *(She goes close as if to caress his cheeks, but slaps him instead.)*
I faith thou hast such reddish cheeks
Thou must have found it hard
I shall forgive when thou dost give
Thy chocolates and card.

ROMEO: Alas my Love, sweet Valentine
Thy card I have it lost
Thy chocolates too *(aside)* Well that's not true
But have you seen the cost?

JULIET: *(Despair turns to anger.)*
No hope, no heart, NO CHOCOLATES!
Fie Romeo, tis undone
No more am I your Juliet
Go find another one.

(She leaves him to wallow in despair.)

THE GOSSIP

(The table is laid. A teapot in a knitted cosy, milk bottle without a lid and a mug. Sydney is slurping his tea from a pint pot as he reads the paper. Agnes enters. She puts down her Bible and pours herself a drink.)

SYDNEY: Ave yer been ter church then, lass?

AGNES: I 'ave that..... I see Ethel wasn't there again.

SYDNEY: No?

AGNES: No..... I don't like to say anything but I heard the vicar talking to her last week and she's got a problem.....

SYDNEY: Oh?

AGNES: Gossiping.

SYDNEY: *(Knowingly.)* Oh.

AGNES: Yes, poor love..... I knew all along of course; I could tell she was a gossiper..... Why just last week ..... in the Butchers ..... she was there telling them how Ernie had got his back problem again and how he should retire! "Ethel," I said, "that's none of your business and you shouldn't be talking about it. You'll be telling them he's going to hospital next - and that's a secret! You just can't keep quiet, can you?"

SYDNEY: No.....

AGNES: "The tongue's a fire," I said. "Just think, just THINK what a large forest can be set on fire by a tiny flame!..... You want to tame the tongue," I said, "and keep it out of other folk's business." *(Sydney slurps loudly.)* Sydney, don't slurp! *(He is about to speak, but she is off again.)*

Wilma Hodgkins was there! I don't know how she dared show her face after last week! ..... I don't like to say anything but ..... she's got a problem .....

BOTH: Gossiping.

AGNES: I say, are you listenin'?

SYDNEY: Ay ..... Yes luv.

AGNES: I suppose I'd best clear these pots since you won't do it ..... sitting there daydreaming. You sit around too much, doing nothing, that's your trouble. You want to get out more ..... It wouldn't do you any harm to come to church with me. You know there's a lot of good sense in that book.

SYDNEY: What book?

AGNES: The Bible. *(She begins to clear away.)*

SYDNEY: Bible eh? *(Picks it up and flicks through.)* I've read some o' that.

AGNES: Really?

SYDNEY: I can quote it too.

AGNES: I'm glad to hear it. *(She is on the way to the kitchen but pauses to hear a quote.)*

SYDNEY: *(Philosophises to audience.)* Better to live on the corner of a roof, than share a house with a nagging wife.....
(Agnes has heard. She turns slowly and advances, picking up the newspaper on the way and rolling it up ready to hit him. Sydney realises what he has done and frantically flicks over the pages for some words of wisdom.)
(Reads.) Enjoy life while you can ..... *(sees her advancing)* ..... Remember, no matter how long you live ..... You'll be dead a lot longer!

(She raises the paper. He cowers. Both freeze.)

LET'S WORK TOGETHER

(This is based on 1 Cor. 12 "The hand cannot say to the eye 'I don't need you' ..... Every part of the body must co-operate to give the best answer to the problem.")

EYE: *..... Carries a ball - an eyeball which is normal on one side, and bloodshot on the other. She wears a belt with an eye on it. It has a compartment in which to keep a string of tears.*

BRAIN: *..... Has a large brain + big ears.*

LOUDMOUTH: *..... Has "loud" lipstick and "loud" clothes. On her feet are teeth, not shoes.*

BRAIN: What have you got there, eye?

EYE: It's an eyeball. I keep it as a spare. A friend gave it to me. I met him when I wore my new mascara. I guess I just caught his eye.

BRAIN: *(Listens.)* Can you hear that?

EYE: What?

BRAIN: There's someone crying.

EYE: Where?

BRAIN: *(Looks around.)* I don't know. I can't see her.

EYE: Oh ..... Yes, I see her. I can see her now. Over there. *(Shows Brain.)* Yes, she's definitely crying. What do you think, Brain?

BRAIN: *(Thinks!)* She's pretty upset. Maybe she needs someone to talk to. I'm a good listener.

EYE: Then why don't you go and talk to her?

BRAIN: I couldn't.

EYE: Go on, Brain ..... You'll think of just the right thing.

BRAIN: No..... No..... I can't go looking like this ..... I'd scare her.

EYE: Nah ..... You're armless!

BRAIN: *(Looks puzzled at arms.)* It's no good. I can't do it. I'd just dry up. I'm no good at talking. .....I know ..... We'll ask Loudmouth.

12

EYE:	She talks all the time!
BOTH:	LOUDMOUTH!
LOUDMOUTH:	*(Enters.)* YEAH?
BRAIN:	Loudmouth, we need your help. We've got a girl here who is crying and she needs some words of sympathy.
LOUDMOUTH:	*(Pleased with herself.)* Oh, oh words! I'm good with words ..... Let's see now ..... *(approaches the girl.)* Dear, dear, ... *(Pleased that they were the right words, then continues.)* What a mess you look! You know, if you don't stop crying your eyes are going to go all red and blotchy .....
EYE:	Like this *(turns eyeball to bloodshot.)*
LOUDMOUTH:	..... And your hair will go all straggly.
BRAIN:	No, no Mouth! You can't talk to her like that! You've got to speak with feeling!
LOUDMOUTH:	*(Offended.)* FEELING! That's not my department! I just say the words ..... You can find your own feeling!
BRAIN:	You're shouting again.
LOUDMOUTH:	Of course I'm shouting; I'm a loudmouth, that's why! What are you getting at me for? You asked me to talk to the girl and I did, didn't I?
EYE:	Yes, but you said all the wrong things! You put your foot in it!
LOUDMOUTH:	*(Even more offended.)* I did NOT put my foot in it. I HAVE NO FEET!
EYE:	*(Looks.)* Oh, I see.
BRAIN:	I think the girl needs sympathy.
LOUDMOUTH:	I can't give sympathy ..... I haven't got a heart! *(Pause. She didn't mean to say that - it was a secret. Now she feels embarrassed and hurt.)* There ..... now you know. *(Embarrassment turns to anger.)* How do you expect me to feel if I HAVE NO HEART?
BRAIN:	*(To Eye.)* Sounds angry to me.
LOUDMOUTH:	*(Angrily.)* ANGRY?
EYE:	*(Goes behind Brain for protection.)* Yes. Very angry.

LOUDMOUTH: *(She goes up to Brain and raises her hand to strike them. They cower. She suddenly stops.)*
Hey ..... You're right! I'm angry ..... I FEEL ANGRY! It's wonderful! ..... Oh it's ..... It's such a strong feeling ..... I've never felt this way before ..... It's ..... I ..... I'm beginning to see!

EYE: Hey, that's MY department!

LOUDMOUTH: Don't you realise what this means? ..... I've got a heart! I can feel! I've got a heart ..... It must be here somewhere ..... *(She starts to search for her heart. She comes across a box - a small chest. The heart is inside. She picks it up, but does not open it.)* Oh, I'm beginning to remember .....

BRAIN: No memories! That's strictly for the Brain! I demand that you stop thinking immediately!

LOUDMOUTH: I can't stop. I remember now. I locked it away a long time ago .....
(Pause. Brain and Eye listen.)
Well I ..... I got hurt you see ..... I thought if I hid it away I couldn't be hurt anymore .....

BRAIN: *(Has a Brainwave!)* STOP! Stop. I have the answer. I know what to do. *(Points to crying girl.)* This girl is sad, right? ..... And we can't cheer her up ..... but she's feeling sad because she's got a heart, so all we have to do is RRRIP IT OUT ..... and she won't feel anymore. It's logical! ..... Then she'll be happy!

EYE: Then she'll be dead!

BRAIN: It's only like locking it away!
(To Loudmouth.) Think! ..... No, don't think ..... I'll think. Listen! No, that's my job too. Look.

EYE: DON'T LOOK!
(To Brain.) If she starts looking I'm leaving. There's nothing else for me to do round here.
(Loudmouth has not been listening. She has been thinking about the contents of the box. Now she wants to open it.)

BRAIN: *(Warns her.)* If you take that heart out you could be hurt again you know. A foot might come along and trample all over it. *(She hesitates, then opens the box, much to Brain's frustration, and takes out the heart.)*

LOUDMOUTH: *(Quietly, to the heart.)* Oh, I've missed you so much ..... It's lovely to see you again.

EYE: *(Insulted.)* I'm warning you ..... *(Points to her belt.)* Eye quit! *(She moves to be on her own and sulks.)*

LOUDMOUTH: Oh Brain ..... I wish you could have a heart too ..... then you could help people more.

BRAIN: I was just trying to solve the problem, that's all! I don't see why she couldn't live without a heart; a lot of people try it.

LOUDMOUTH: BUT THEY'RE DEAD! ..... Dead ..... Dead inside.
(Pause. Loudmouth is upset.)

BRAIN: Oh, now don't you start. Don't cry on me.

LOUDMOUTH: I'm sorry. I feel so sad. I just want to cry.

EYE: Aha! I knew I'd come in useful. *(She is gloating in her triumph.)* Here we go ..... *(She unravels the string of teardrops to fall from the eye on her belt. She shows them off as if it is the latest fashion.)*

LOUDMOUTH: I feel so sorry for all those people ..... You know, I even feel sorry for that poor girl. *(Pause.)*
Whole people! We should be whole people, Brain! Why don't we know when something's missing? Why didn't I realise I had a hole where my heart should be? *(To Eye.)* I couldn't see!

EYE: ..... Whole people ..... I want to be whole too, Loudmouth. I don't want to be an eye anymore. I'm so useless on my own ..... I daren't get involved in anything - I just stand back and watch it all ..... and if I see a problem, Loudmouth, I just look somewhere else .....

BRAIN: You think you've got problems! Look at these ears! I hear everything but what do I do about it? I just THINK! ..... I'm so busy thinking, I never even see when people need help.

EYE: There's one over there that needs help. *(Pause.)*

LOUDMOUTH: Come on ..... We're in this together.
(They all go to the girl and assume a kind, understanding pose.)

THE PRICE IS PAID

(This sketch is based on Romans 5 ..... While we were still sinners Christ died for us. The Sheriff enjoys his authority. The Stranger has a husky voice and a poncho. He may be quiet, but he must also be strong. The scene begins with a solemn drumbeat. William Morton, a cardboard cut out, is brought on and stood in place to face his judgement.)

JOSH: *(Excited.)* This here's court, an' you awl better quieten down now, we got us a trial!

SHERIFF: William Morton, you is charged with shootin', killin', conspirin' to do evil .....

JOSH: Evil .....

SHERIFF: ..... an' lyin' ..... You is guilty man, an' you're gonna pay.

JOSH: That's right Sherreef - You make him pay now, d'yer hear?

SHERIFF: An' you hol yer tongue Josh Wakefield ..... I's about to lay sentence. See here Morton, you'se about the guiltiest man I ever did know, and I hereby place on you, by the authority bestowed upon me, the death penalty. Take him away boy an' hang him.
(Josh gets hold of the cut-out. The Stranger enters.)

STRANGER: STOP!
(They both stop in their tracks and look.)

SHERIFF: What the? ..... Oh, it's the new kid in town. Reckon you don't know how we do things round here mister.

JOSH: Yeah ..... We's administerin' justice, ain't we Sherreef?

SHERIFF: We sure are Josh, we sure are.

STRANGER: I know he's guilty.

SHERIFF: Well then you don't mind if we jest get on now, do yer?
(Josh gets hold of William again.)

STRANGER: I said I know he's guilty ..... I know he done wrong, but you can take me. Kill me instead.
(They both stop in their tracks again.)

SHERIFF: What the? ..... Ain't that jest about the craziest thing you ever did hear Josh?

JOSH: Sure is Sherreef ..... Why, he must ha lost his raisins talkin' like that.

16

STRANGER: Let him live ..... you can take me. *(Pause.)*

SHERIFF: Now if you're gonna keep on talkin' like that you're gonna get yourself a whole lot of trouble - I might jest believe yer.

JOSH: Yeah ..... You're a genuine hero, ain't yer? ..... Pity you're gonna be a dead one! Ha ha ha .....

STRANGER: A man's godda do what a man's godda do.
(This line scares Josh. The Sheriff is disgusted. They eye each other as if there's going to be a shoot out. The Sheriff takes his cigar our of his mouth and blows smoke in the Stranger's face, then wheezes - he overdid it.)

SHERIFF: You talk too much, boy. Reckon we don't like your face around here.
(He takes the Stranger's cowboy hat off, drops it, treads on it, then jumps on it. He appears to be apologetic.)
Oh dear, oh my ..... Oh now ain't that a shame? I jest trodden on your hat! ..... Pick it up boy.
(The Sheriff has his hand on his holster. Josh moves in close, ready for a fight. The Stranger picks the hat, dusts it down and slowly puts it back on. The Sheriff gets hold of it and turns it, to look silly on the Stranger. Josh laughs.)
Now ain't you a proper cowboy?

JOSH: No Sherreef, he ain't a proper cowboy ..... A proper cowboy has spurs ..... THERE! *(He kicks Stranger's shins.)*

SHERIFF: Yeah, an' a proper cowboy has a gun, like this one.
(He produces a toy gun and threatens the Stranger.)

JOSH: An' a proper cowboy fights back when he's pushed. (Pushes him.)

SHERIFF: Reckon this ain't no proper cowboy then.

JOSH: No, but he's a hero ..... *(Shows contempt.)* wants to die fer somebody else .....

SHERIFF: You'll get your wish mister .....
(They push, thump and eventually twist his arms in such a way as to form a crucifix. Although the Stranger does not resist, there are groans of pain. They hold the crucifix position. When they let go the Stranger falls to the ground, dead. They are nervous and shocked at what they have done.) (Pause.)

SHERIFF: *(To the cut-out.)* Morton, you can go ..... Your price is paid.

THE GOOD SAMARITAN

(Mr. Wiseman is very clever. He manipulates Mr. Really Stupid all the time, yet Mr. Really Stupid does not realise it. Mr. Wiseman is an accomplished actor, so should show convincing characters and also have his own character well established. Mr. Really Stupid is easily confused, but always tries to enjoy things.)

(Mr. Wiseman addresses the audience. Mr. Really Stupid is standing in the background in suitable pose, listening in on the speech.)

MR. WISEMAN:	This evening I should like to tell you the story of The Good Samaritan, ... but alas ..... I cannot.
MR. REALLY STUPID:	Oh *(sad.)*
MR. WISEMAN:	If only I had a friend to help me act it out but that is not possible - to do this part he would have to be Really Stupid!
MR. REALLY STUPID:	Oh! *(Enthusiastic.)* Hello Mr. Wiseman.
MR. WISEMAN:	*(Feigned surprise.)* OH, hello Mr. ..... er .....
MR. REALLY STUPID:	Really Stupid!
MR. WISEMAN:	Yes.
MR. REALLY STUPID:	Can I help?
MR. WISEMAN:	Well .....
MR. REALLY STUPID:	Oh, go on .....
MR. WISEMAN:	All right ..... One day, a man was walking along ..... *(Mr. Really Stupid smiles and walks along. Though his body walks to the right, and then to the left, his face is always forward.)* When suddenly, a nasty vicious gangster appeared. *(Mr. Wiseman plays the gangster.)* Hey, you ..... You're not from round here.
MR. REALLY STUPID:	No. I live over at ..... you know where I live!
MR. WISEMAN:	*(Takes him aside. Whispers.)* I'm acting.
MR. REALLY STUPID:	What?
MR. WISEMAN:	I'm acting the part of a vicious gangster.
MR. REALLY STUPID:	Oh ..... You're very good.

MR. WISEMAN:	Thank you.
	(They resume the scene.)
	I don't like your face, stranger.
MR. REALLY STUPID:	Stranger. *(He realises he is to play the part.)*
MR. WISEMAN:	Think I'll shape it up a little.
MR. REALLY STUPID:	*(Indignant.)* Are you threatening me?
MR. WISEMAN:	Yes.
MR. REALLY STUPID:	*(Crumbles.)* Oooooh!
MR. WISEMAN:	*(Calls.)* Bring on the sheet! .....
	(To audience.) I hate to see violence.
MR. REALLY STUPID:	*(Cringing and begging.)* Oh so do I ..... so do I!

(Two smiling people bring on a sheet and hold it in front of the men. Mr. Wiseman puts his hand on Mr. Really Stupid's head and pushes him down out of view. There is the sound of groans, thumps, pain, and the sheet moves showing there is a fight behind it. Now and then cards appear above the sheet. They say - BIFF! WHACK! POW! Mr. Really Stupid's head appears above the sheet, but a hand pulls him back down. Eventually, Mr. Really Stupid keels over backwards in view. Mr. Wiseman stands up, smiling. He holds up the final card - SPLAT! The sheet is taken away. Mr. Really Stupid groans. Mr. Wiseman now plays a vicar passing by. He goes over and studies Mr. Really Stupid.)

MR. WISEMAN:	Nasty ..... very nasty.
	(He lifts his friend half way up - as if to help him get up.)
	(To audience.) This is what you get when you join the wrong crowd.
	(He lets go. Mr. Really Stupid falls again.)
	Tut tut tut ..... the youth of today!
	(He leaves, and returns as Mr. Wiseman.)
MR. WISEMAN:	Poor Mr. Really Stupid! *(He helps him up.)* Looks like someone gave you a beating!
MR. REALLY STUPID:	It was you ..... It was you!
MR. WISEMAN:	Ah ..... yes ..... I always say "If a job's worth doing - it's worth doing well". Come on ..... let's bandage the bit that hurts. *(He bandages his head.)*

MR. REALLY STUPID: It's me leg ..... It's me leg!

MR. WISEMAN: Never mind. *(Produces card.)* I know a sweet kind lady who will look after you, bandage your wounds and see that you're all right. I'll pay the bill! It's over there. *(He points.)*

MR. REALLY STUPID: Over there. *(He points, but does not look.)*

MR. WISEMAN: Bye.

MR. REALLY STUPID: Bye. *(He turns to go and looks.)* ..... but that's MY house! ..... And I'm all dirty ..... my wife'll kill me! ..... Oooooh! I need some help. *(He takes out a pocket Bible and reads.)* "Do not worry." ..... Do NOT worry ..... Do NOT WORRY! ..... Wife ..... Mrs Really Stupid, Dear!

(Freeze.)

THE GOOD HOUSEWIFE'S GUIDE TO CHRISTMAS

(Scene. Mum is seated watching telly. The kids are frozen in an arguing pose. The Narrator is beaming from behind her desk.)

NARRATOR: Good evening. You are watching "THE GOOD HOUSEWIFE'S GUIDE TO CHRISTMAS". The secret of good preparation is a quiet, roomy house, so ..... step one - get rid of the kids.

MUM: *(To kids.)* OUTSIDE!

NARRATOR: They'll just love it outside, playing in the snow.

KATE: Mum, it's freezing outside!

MUM: You can wrap up warm, you can put your scarf on.

KATE: No mum ..... it's all right .....

MUM: I knitted it for you and I never see you wearing it.
(Mum wraps scarf round her and tucks it in. Kate feels stupid. Julie points and laughs. They go outside.)

KATE: Just you wait.
(She makes a snowball and throws it. Direct hit.)

JULIE: OW! Mum ..... mum ..... look what she's done to me.

KATE: She started it.

MUM: INSIDE. *(They go inside.)* ..... and take your boots ..... off.
(It is too late - the carpet is dirty.)

NARRATOR: Now we can begin our cake with our favourite recipe using the all-in-one method.
(Mum puts an apron on. The Narrator demonstrates, and mum copies. The Narrator's actions are professional; mum clumsily picks big handfuls and drops them into the basin. The kids are bored and play catch.)
Just add a bit of this, a bit of that, and a touch of brandy .....
(One of the kids bumps into mum whilst she is adding the brandy. The cake receives a generous portion. The kids run off stage.)
..... and mix it all in.
(Narrator mixes easily; mum is grinding the wooden spoon with severe arm-ache.)
..... While the cake is happily cooking you have a couple of hours to turn your attention to wrapping the surprise

presents.
(Mum gets the present and paper, etc. She is ready to wrap, but hides present as Kate enters.)

KATE: Mum, have you seen my earrings?

MUM: No.
(She leaves. Mum tries again.)

JULIE: *(Enters.)* Mum, can I bring some friends round tonight?

MUM: *(Hiding present.)* Of course you can. Bring them for tea ..... Is it Emma and Sarah again?

JULIE: No mum, it's the youth group.
(Julie leaves. Mum tries again.)

KATE: *(Enters.)* Oh great! I've been looking for these!
(She takes the scissors and paper.)

NARRATOR: Don't forget our healthy economy spot.
A pound of Freddy's X BRAND mincemeat
A pound of polyunsaturated X BRAND margarine
Two pounds of wholegrain brown X BRAND flour and a spot of fully skimmed goat milk
This makes 72 mince pies for under a pound!
(Mum gives pie to kids. They take a bite and show their disgust. Freeze.)
..... and they last a long time too!
Of course, for that personal touch, you should give home-made presents.
(The kids mime "No" behind mum's back since she is listening intently.)
Sewing is a useful skill, and you can make some garments quite easily.
(The kids are in despair. Mum is taking notes.)
Perhaps you have some old material which can be transformed into a new outfit.
(Mum produces some horrifically outdated material. The kids look at it and faint onto each other.)
On Christmas day, a tidy home is a happy home. Make a special effort to create a peaceful environment.
(NOISE! The kids rip open Christmas presents. All paper goes on the floor.)

MUM: Pick it up!

JULIE: She dropped it.

KATE: No I didn't.

JULIE: Yes you did.

KATE: *(Holds chocolate out.)* Want a chocolate?

JULIE: Yes.

KATE: So do I *(She stuffs it in.)*
             (Mum clears up the mess whilst the kids settle to watch telly. Kate eats chocolate after chocolate.)

NARRATOR: After the Christmas dinner, put your feet up and relax - watch the film; the kids'll do the washing up.
             (Mum claps and points to the sink. No response. She resigns herself to it and washes the pots.)

KATE: Mom ..... I feel sick.
             (Freeze.)

NARRATOR: After being .....

KATE: Nurse.
             (Mum brings bucket over.)

JULIE: Mum.

KATE: Hostess.
             (Mum produces cup of water.)

JULIE: Cook. *(Julie grimaces and holds stomach. Mum sees and is offended.)*

KATE: And cleaner.
             (Mum takes the bucket away.)

NARRATOR: The sad time will come when all your aunts, uncles, friends and relatives will have to leave.

MUM & KIDS: Bye ..... bye ..... see yer ..... bye .....
             (Kids go to play with their presents. Mum just stands.)

NARRATOR: But don't forget the one who is left behind .....
             (Mum wipes her hand over her hair, leaving it a tangled mess and staggers to a chair where she sits, shattered.)
             ..... your husband. Now is the time to look beautiful; just for him.
             (Mum does not react to anything now.)

JULIE: Mum, can I play with the Monopoly now?

KATE: No. I want to watch the late night film.

JULIE: I asked first.

KATE:	You can play Monopoly anytime ..... Mum .....
JULIE:	I want to play it now.
KATE:	Mum .....
JULIE:	Dad - tell her I asked first.
KATE:	Dad, why can't I see the film? It is Christmas!
JULIE:	Dad, will you play Monopoly with me?
KATE:	Dad, tell Mum I can stay up late ..... It is Christmas!

(They leave, pursuing Dad.   Mum is still seated, bedraggled.)

THE SCHEDULE

(A kind, patient, "I know about these things" person has drawn up a schedule to bring order into Jesus' chaotic life. This is a sketch for all those people who are constantly frustrated that events don't happen neatly at their proper time and end up in a lot of "last minute" circumstances. The organiser can talk to an empty chair imagining Jesus' replies. He/she begins by being pleasant and understanding; after all, the idea is so good it is bound to be accepted.)

VOICE: If you don't mind me saying so Lord, you could do with a bit more organisation. I mean - crowds everywhere! All wanting to see you at once ..... Tell me, when was the last time we had dinner at dinner-time? ..... Exactly! Now if you'd just let me manage your schedule things would be a lot more efficient.

(The person proceeds to be efficient.)

Look, I've drawn up a list so you can see how you like it.
First thing in the morning - Healings.
There's a paralysed man
One deaf
One blind
And one with a bad hand.
I would have left it at that but we had a Roman official with a sick child. I thought you ought to slip that one in.

That takes you up to break ..... (Jesus looks puzzled.)
Coffee break! ..... It's your right you know; you should take it. I've made an appointments list for people to see you so that we don't keep people waiting. There was a tax collector but I didn't think you'd want him on the list. There was a bunch of kids hanging around too but I got rid of them. After all, we want to talk seriously, don't we?

I thought of finding a hall for you to speak in too ..... Yes I know more people can fit on the hill but it must be hard on your voice out there.

You see we could organise sessions so that everyone goes home at a reasonable time and you get a rest ..... They have to eat sometime you know! ..... Didn't I see the boy today? ..... The one that offered to share his dinner? .....Oh yeah ..... five loaves and two fishes! That'll never be enough.

So, what do you think of the schedule then? (Offended.) You don't like it ..... But I wanted to give you a break, that's all!

"My Father is always working and so must I" ..... I see.

Well, I can't stop you, but I think my idea is a lot more convenient!

ANY MINUTE NOW

(The compere sets the scene with an air of anticipation. Ethel reacts as if she has just won a holiday in Bermuda.)

COMPERE: Any minute now some poor, unsuspecting customer is going to come here, to shop.
(Ethel enters carrying her shopping basket.)
CONGRATULATIONS! You are our hundred and forty-seventh customer, coming here to shop, and you win..... ABSOLUTELY NOTHING!

ETHEL: Oooh! *(She is overwhelmed.)*

COMPERE: Did you have any idea that today would be such an ORDINARY day?

ETHEL: *(Delighted.)* Well, I must admit I had an inkling. ..... When I burnt the toast this morning I thought to myself: "Ethel, this is going to be one of those BORING, run-of-the-mill days." *(She is enjoying the limelight.)*

COMPERE: And tell me Ethel, how do you feel?

ETHEL: Oh, very happy to be just one of the crowd.

COMPERE: And has this experience changed you at all?

ETHEL: Oh no, not a bit! *(At first she thinks he means will fame go to her head, then slowly the truth dawns and she becomes deflated.)*

COMPERE: Well, I must let you get to the check-out and pay for your tin of beans ..... just like you do every week.

ETHEL: Th..... Thankyou. *(She is confused. The compere steers her towards the counter. She goes.)*

COMPERE: So there we have it, ladies and gentlemen..... There goes another ORDINARY person who has had NO LIFE-CHANGING EXPERIENCE!

FEED THE FIRE

(Two actors talk as they set up the scene. The first one is disgruntled; he is sure he will be in trouble.)

1:    .....Let me get this straight ..... We're supposed to be doing a sketch about church, so you've written about trains.

2:    I couldn't think of one about church.

1:    So why are we up here?

2:    We were asked to do a sketch.

1:    Yes, but I think they meant a <u>relevant</u> one!

2:    I couldn't think of a relevant one!

1:    *(Despairing.)* Oh boy! Are we in for it after the service! *(Disgusted.)* A sketch about church! .....

2:    Look! If we just get on with it no-one will notice.

1:    *(Perks up.)* That's true!

      (They start the sketch.)

PASSENGER: (1) Lovely TRAIN!

DRIVER: (2) Yes. Lovely TRAIN.

PASSENGER: Plush seating.

DRIVER: Big windows.

PASSENGER: Oh, beautiful windows!

DRIVER: There's a buffet car, you know .....

PASSENGER: Really? *(Gets up to go.)*

DRIVER: But it's not open until we get moving.

PASSENGER: *(Sits down.)* I prefer the other sort myself ..... where the waiter brings the tea round.

DRIVER: Now that's service!

PASSENGER: Yes. You don't even have to get out of your chair. ..... Actually I wanted to be on a sleeper, but there was just no room.

DRIVER: No. They're very popular.

      (Pause.)

      These new models go very fast when they get started, you know..... Just wait till we're out of the station; hundred miles an hour in seconds! If you blink you'll miss the view. All that power at the touch of a button.

      (Pause.)

PASSENGER:	Rodney.....
DRIVER:	Yes.
PASSENGER:	Something's missing.
DRIVER:	Is there? *(Checks.)* Tickets ..... seats ..... *(Gleefully.)* Paper..... *(He is ready to read.)*
PASSENGER:	The view! The view! We're still in the station.
DRIVER:	Not for long. The Station Master's out there blowing his whistle. That means we can go.
PASSENGER:	He's been blowing his whistle for the last five minutes. What's stopping us?
DRIVER:	Give it time ..... *(They watch out of the window.)* What's he doing now?
PASSENGER:	He's waving his arms..... He's waving at you! Does he know you?
DRIVER:	Probably seen me around. *(They watch.)* What's he doing now?
PASSENGER:	He's shouting..... *(Puzzled.)* "Start the engine" .....
DRIVER:	Huh! Giving orders now, are we? *(Shouts back.)* Not me mate..... I'm just a passenger..... I'm not moving.
PASSENGER:	Nor is the train.
	(They look at each other briefly.)
DRIVER:	I remember the old days. Steam engines! Now they were trains! Massive, majestic, powerful. They took some getting going though.
PASSENGER:	*(Disapproves.)* All that coal.
DRIVER:	Shovels.
PASSENGER:	Dirt.
DRIVER:	Muscles.
PASSENGER:	Sweat.
DRIVER:	Wussles.
PASSENGER:	Wussles?
DRIVER:	Whistle didn't rhyme, did it?

(Much to the embarrassment of the passenger, the driver becomes carried away, imitating a train.)

(Whistle) Woooh woooh! *(Passenger looks at him.)*
(Slowly) Feed the fire, feed the fire,
(Quicker) Feed the fire, feed the fire,
(Pace) Feed the fire and shovel it in,

Feed the fire and shovel it in,
Shovel it in, shovel it in,
Shovel it in, shovel it in,
WOOOH, WOOOOOH!

(*Steam*) Pssssssssssssssh.

(*Excited.*) By, they could move! You saw some scenery then. Marvellous!

PASSENGER: What happened?

DRIVER: Too much like hard work ..... and messy. I spent ALL MY DAYS in an oily old boiler suit. The wife wasn't too keen.

PASSENGER: But you enjoyed it.

DRIVER: Aye, back in the OLD days! When I had more energy, you know! I'm not going to start all that again now! It's all GREEN now. I've joined the Conservation Party.

PASSENGER: What's that?

DRIVER: Dedicated to the Conservation of Energy. Where's my paper? (*He settles down to read ..... Looks up.*)
Well don't just stand there! Take a seat. Relax. Enjoy the view.

PASSENGER: ..... of the station. (*Frustrated.*)

(*Pause.*)

(*Driver reads. Passenger stares out of the window.*)

PASSENGER: The Master's still blowing his whistle. Actually, he's blowing the whistle, waving a flag, jumping up and down and looking quite frustrated.

DRIVER: I can't understand it. (*Puts his driver's cap on. Passenger stares at it. Driver looks at his watch.*) Dinner time. No point in setting off now. I'm off home. See you next week, same train.

(*The sketch is over. They pack up.*)

2: That wasn't too bad.

1: No.

2: I don't think they noticed.

1: No.

2: Next time, don't call me Rodney.

LOOKING FOR DIRECTION?

(A man asks directions of three passers by.)

MAN: Excuse me ..... I'm lost.

1:      Visitor, eh?

MAN: No. I've lived here all my life. *(The Man hasn't heard.)*

1:      ..... A traveller on that great highway of life, stopping to visit our humble town. Can't think why. There's nothing to see. What do you want, Mate?

MAN: I want to be happy.

1:      Oh well, then you want the Happy Hour down at the "Duck n' Rabbit". Go up here, turn left, turn left and turn left again and it's in front of you.

MAN: But that brings me back where I started.

1:      Yes. It's over the road. Be happy! *(Exit.)*

(Number 2 walks by.)

MAN: Excuse me ..... I don't mean to trouble you with my problems but I'm lost.

2:      What do you want?

MAN: I want to be free.

2:      You want America! Sun, sea and action. You can't beat it. I've been surfin' on the waves, been round the nightclubs ..... A real "Get-away-from-it-all". I've just been for a fortnight.

MAN: But now you're back.

2:      Yeah. Dreams don't last forever. The Travel Agents is right, right and right again. *(He tries to leave.)*

MAN: No you don't understand ..... I'm lost!

2:      *(His patience is waning.)* Where do you want to go?

MAN: I don't know! I don't really have any direction.

2:      You need a good job. One with promotion; give you something to aim for.

MAN: *(Frustrated.)* I've had promotion!

2:      That's it then! You're doing fine! You have all the marks of success. More money .....

MAN:	..... More work, more business trips, more bills, more responsibility, more deadlines, MORE STRESS .....
2:	You need to relax. Try the Gym. Turn left, then right then over the bridge, cross at the traffic lights, go down the underground, turn right and right again, take the second left and it's on your right ..... That enough direction?
MAN:	*(Depressed.)* Thanks.
	(Number 2 leaves, relieved. Number 3 enters.)
	Excuse me ..... I'm lost.
3:	What do you want?
MAN:	*(Desperate.)* I want to be found.
3:	*(Thinks.)* Er - the Police Station is on your left .....
MAN:	No, not literally speaking, <u>mentally</u> speaking .....
3:	*(Confused.)* The Hospital's on your .....
MAN:	NO! Why can no-one UNDERSTAND ME? Please ..... please ..... I've met so many people and they can't tell me where to go. I've been to all the places they can think of but I still have this strong feeling that I'm missing something.
3:	Sorry mate - that's life!
	(Number 3 is glad to leave. The man is now totally depressed. A timid number 4 appears and approaches him.)
4:	Excuse me ..... I wonder if you could help me? I'm lost.
MAN:	What do you want?
4:	I want to be happy.
MAN:	*(With no enthusiasm.)* Try the Happy Hour at the "Duck n' Rabbit". It's up there, turn left, turn left again ..... *(Fade out.)*

(If you do not wish to end the sketch in such a serious mood you can lighten it with this. The monologue can be half sung, half spoken by someone neurotic. You could have an "Oom Pah oom pah" piano accompaniment in the background!)

MAN:

I can worry about money
I can worry about life
I can drive myself quite silly
When I worry 'bout my wife.

I can worry 'bout promotion
But it's tough up at the top
Will they give me a demotion?
Will this worry ever stop?

All this worry makes me weary
So I try to catch a nap
As my eyesight goes all bleary
Worry has me in its trap.

For I dream those situations
And they tell me I'm in stress
So I quickly lose my patience
Then I'm really in a mess!

First I worry 'bout the future
Then I worry 'bout the past
If I get a bit of peace
I worry how long it will last.

You know I try to do things right
But then I worry if I'm wrong
Will I ever sleep tonight?
Will I ever end this song?

Someone has to help me fast
And tell my worrying to cease
Or I'll worry till my last
And hope that then I'll rest in peace.

THE DEATH SCENE

(Played in melodramatic style. A wounded soldier in full armour staggers on stage and crawls along, arms reaching out.)

SOLDIER: *(Groan.)* Mercy.....mercy ..... water.....water .....
(Lady appears.)
At last! Refuge..... Refuge from the war.

LADY: My warrior - wounded!

SOLDIER: Tis but a flesh wound. *(Sees she is concerned and plays the rest as if it were a major piece of drama.)*
..... Though it may become INFECTED and spread through the WHOLE BODY ..... until I DIE!

LADY: Then I shall tend to it at once.

SOLDIER: Not yet, fair one ..... Oh speak more words of sympathy first. Pity me - a poor, abandoned, dying soldier.....

LADY: Tis but a cut.

SOLDIER: I know, but why waste a good scene? .....
(He describes his valiant exploits to the audience.)
There I was in battle, fighting for my King; the enemy all around. The forces came against me but I slew them with my trusty sword *(wields sword)* .....
Have you ever tried wielding a sword all day? *(Puffed out.)* These things are heavy! *(He puts it down.)* I walked safe through the THOUSAND arrows with my shield held high from the morn *(Walks on spot 'holding his shield high')* to noon *(lowers shield, staggers)* and the eventide *(puts shield down)* and it gets your shoulder just there! *(Rolls shoulder. It is stiff.)*

LADY: Brave soldier, I will fetch thy cup. Life-giving water shall refresh thee.

SOLDIER: Not yet, I haven't finished the speech. *(Back to the drama.)*
My head..... *(puts hand on helmet)* pounding..... POUNDING! *(Takes helmet off)* with the sound of fire. *(Holds head)* ..... Cries echoing in my mind ..... yet I struggled onward ..... ever onward.

LADY: *(Seriously concerned.)* Drink. I pray thee drink. Be refreshed.

SOLDIER: *(He is engrossed in his own performance. Places hands on hips then looks down and thinks of the belt.)* This belt..... *(Takes it* off *and holds it up.)* This trusty belt has carried sword and dagger on the battlefield. My close companion in a dark hour. .....I offer it thee in token of my love.

LADY: *(No response.)*

SOLDIER: *(Aside.)* That's your cue..... *(prompts her)* "I will give thee water....." *(He waits for her.)*

LADY: No big death scene?

SOLDIER: *(Puzzled and frustrated. This was not in the script.)* Of course no big death scene; it's just a scratch!

LADY: *(No response.)*

SOLDIER: It's ketchup! Taste it! *(Pause.)*

LADY: *(She walks past him, bends down and picks up the sword. She holds it with care.)* The brave warrior lays down his sword, abandons his shield and removes his belt. *(Turns to him.)* Without his armour ..... my soldier will die indeed.
